# Quayside
# and the Chares

by

Jack and John Leslie

Published by

Newcastle Libraries & Information Service

Acknowledgments:

Many thanks to Dilys Harding and the City Library Local Studies Section for their help, and to Ian Ayris and Frank Manders for their invaluable advice.

Edited by Anna Flowers and Vanessa Histon.

Photographic acknowledgements:

All photographs are copyright of Newcastle Libraries & Information Service except for 13a, which is copyright of Newcastle City Council Environmental Health.

ISBN: 1 85795 146 8

©Jack and John Leslie, 2002

City of Newcastle upon Tyne, Education & Libraries Directorate, Newcastle Libraries & Information Service, 2002

Front cover: The Quayside, 1963.

Frontispiece: A detail from Oliver's map of Newcastle upon Tyne, 1830.

A brief selection of further reading:

Ayris, Ian & Sheldon, Patricia, *On the Waterfront: An Historical Tour of Newcastle's Quayside*, Newcastle City Libraries & Arts, 1995.

Barke, M. & Buswell, R.J., *Newcastle's Changing Map*, Newcastle City Libraries & Arts, 1992.

Ed. Grundy, John et al, *The Buildings of England: Northumberland*, Penguin, 1992.

Leslie, Jack and John, *Bygone West Quayside and the Close*, Newcastle Libraries & Information Service, 2001.

Pearson, Lynn, *Northern City: An Architectural History of Newcastle upon Tyne*, Newcastle City Libraries, 1996.

## For your information …

Copies of photographs which are copyright of Newcastle Libraries & Information Service may be ordered and purchased from the Local Studies Section, Newcastle City Library.

City Tours visit the city and suburbs during the Summer months. A free brochure is available from Newcastle Tourist Information Centre (tel: 0191 2778000).

A free brochure detailing other local history publications is also available from Newcastle City Library.

For information on any of the above contact

Tyne Bridge Publishing
City Library
Princess Square
Newcastle upon Tyne
NE99 1DX

or telephone 0191 2774174.

Visit our website at:
www.newcastle.gov.uk/tynebridgepublishing
for all the latest information.

This booklet follows a route from the Guildhall via All Saints to Pandon and Sandgate, and then back to Sandhill along the river frontage.

A brook known as the Lorke or Lort Burn ran down a deep ravine or dene, and entered the Tyne at Sandhill. Nearby was a hospital, the 'Maison Dieu', built in 1412. It was altered and extended into the Guildhall from the 17th century. In 1785, when Dean Street was built, the Lort Burn was filled in on the orders of architect David Stephenson.

In 1298 the part of the town wall running from Carliol Croft down to the river was diverted further to the to the east at Corner Tower to include the Pandon township. The new section of the wall stretched through Pandon Dene to Sallyport Tower and down to the river at Sandgate. Pandon Burn flowed from the north of the town around to the east through rolling meadows to the river near Broad Chare. Two of the burn's crossings, Barras Bridge and New Bridge, are still street names.

The Sandgate area was built on sand like much of the lower part of the town. It was once closely linked with river trade and the shipwrights and keelmen who lived in the narrow alleys of this area are remembered in many Newcastle folk songs, such as *The Keel Row*.

Before the Swing Bridge was opened in 1876, sea-going ships could only navigate the river as far as the old Tyne Bridge. Coal was brought downstream to the river mouth from the collieries in flat bottomed boats known as keels and loaded onto coal ships for transport to ports all over Britain and Europe. Keelmen did not go to sea. Mackenzie in his *History of Northumberland* described the keelmen who operated the keel boats as being 'more robust than any other tribe in England'. The keelmen had a strong sense of brotherhood, and in 1701 they funded the building and maintenance of their own hospital for the old and infirm near Sandgate. As the navigability of the Tyne improved, the keelmen lost their trade and by 1872 the Society of Keelmen had been abolished.

From Medieval times chares or narrow alleys extended from the Quayside between Sandhill and Broad Chare. They had names reflecting their appearance or residents, such as Dark Chare, Blue Anchor Chare, Peppercorn Chare, Fenwick's Entry and Love Lane. Names might change over the years, including Armourer's Chare, which became Colvin Chare. By the mid 19th century the chares had become run down and insanitary. The wealthy merchants, seeking cleaner, lighter living conditions had moved out of the area, leaving it to poorer residents who had no choice other than these dark, cramped conditions. Typhus was endemic. There were cholera epidemics in 1831-2, and 1848-9. In the 1853 epidemic over 1,500 people, many living on the Quayside, lost their lives.

On Friday 6 October 1854 a catastrophic fire destroyed many of the chares (see photograph 18). After the fire new streets were laid out, and with Victorian redevelopment, the Quayside became predominantly commercial.

However, the business centre of Newcastle gradually moved away from the cramped Quayside towards higher ground. The opening of the road deck of the the High Level Bridge in 1850 and the Tyne Bridge in 1928 diverted most traffic to the upper part of the town, so the Quayside area began to decline.

The Quayside was fairly dilapidated for much of the 20th century, but in the 1990s Newcastle City Council, in partnership with developers, began a sympathetic restoration of many historic buildings on the Quayside. The area has undergone a rebirth, as a focal point for the city's thriving nightlife, as a business centre, and with the building of the magnificent new Law Courts, as an administrative centre.

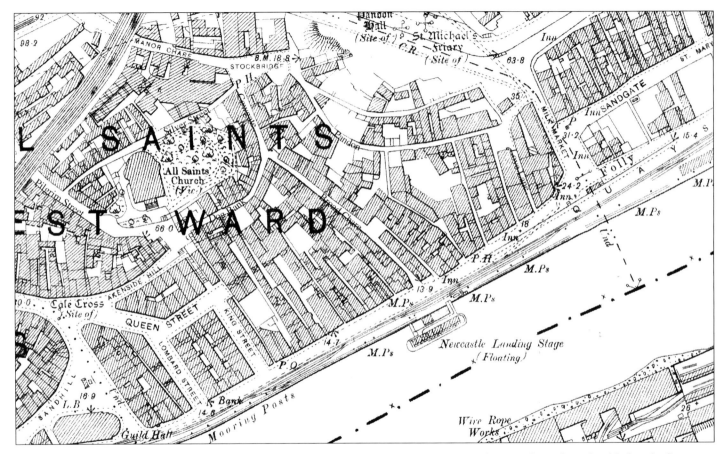

1. The O.S. map of 1898 showing part of the Quayside (with some added street names). The narrow lanes or chares that existed before the fire of 1854 had vanished, and much redevelopment had been carried out by John Dobson. Compare it with the 1830 map shown on the frontispiece where the chares can be seen. Broad Chare and Spicer Lane are just opposite the Floating Landing Stage.

2. The Quayside and Guildhall, 1897. The rounded building with columns at the eastern end of the Guildhall is the Fish Market, designed by John Dobson and opened on 2 January 1826. It replaced the original 'Maison Dieu', where a priest offered care for 'nine poor men and four poor women', and the stalls of the old fish market. It was fitted out with stone benches, one of which was semi-circular and 55ft 6ins long. The building was initially very unpopular with the fishwives who used it.

'The good ladies who presided the stalls seriously objected to being removed from their old quarters, and for some time Mr Dobson received such an impolite reception from them that he was obliged to avoid their presence. But when bad weather came, and they realised the comfort of their new abode, they relented, and a deputation of fair dames arrived at his residence in New Bridge Street with a peace offering of fish for a Christmas dinner. Ever after that he was their cannie Mr Dobson.' (extract from *John Dobson: Architect of the North East* by Thomas Faulkner and Andrew Greg, Tyne Bridge Publishing 2001.)

The building in the foreground is Ye Old Queen Elizabeth Inn, one of the few survivors of the fire of 1854 (see photo 14) and a reminder of the character of the pre-Victorian Quayside.

3. Akenside Hill leads east from the Side. Before the construction of Dean Street, this street was one of the main thoroughfares from the river to the higher parts of the town. Originally known as All Hallows Bank because it ran up to All Hallows Church (later All Saints Church), on Pilgrim Street, its name was later changed to Butcher Bank because of the many butchers' shops on the street.

By 1863 there were no butchers left in the street and the middle-class residents preferred a name more in keeping with their status. Several new names, including Cornhill, were proposed, but the Corporation finally settled on Akenside Hill.

The new name honoured Mark Akenside, a renowned physician and poet, who was born in the street, above his father's shop at 33 Butcher Bank on 9 November 1721. When he was seven years, old a butcher's cleaver fell on his foot leaving him with a permanent limp. According to contemporaries, Akenside did not have a particularly pleasant disposition, and was not proud of his place of birth. Mark Akenside died in 1770 and was interned in St James Church, Westminster.

The photograph shows Akenside Hill in 1925, looking down towards The Side. The cheap lodging house on the right had once been a splendid building, but its dilapidated condition indicates that the middle classes had left the area.

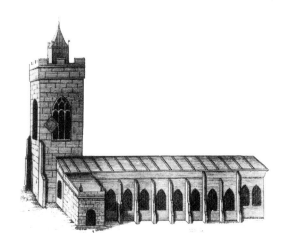

4. All Saints Church has been described as the finest elliptical classical church in the land. A medieval church on this site, All Hallows, had an impressive name: All Hallows Omnium Animarium, Pantown Thewn, derived from the ancient name of Pampeden or Pandon. It had three galleries and contained the tomb of the Newcastle mayor and benefactor Roger Thornton. All Hallows gradually fell into decay, one of the vestry windows falling out in 1753. Eventually, further repairs were deemed too expensive and on Easter Tuesday 18 April 1786, a general meeting of the parishioners unanimously resolved to demolish the church and erect a new one. The foundation stone of All Saints Church was laid on 14 August 1786. Designed by David Stephenson, the elegant new church was completed in 1796 at a cost of £27,000. John Wesley, the founder of Methodism, worshipped in All Saints when he visited Newcastle. The church was declared redundant in 1961, but is now St Willibrord with All Saints, an Anglican Catholic church.

The photograph shows All Saints Church in 1910. The drawing of All Hallows Church is taken from a map of 1723.

5. Silver Street in 1885. This street, which was once known as All Hallows Gate, ran along the north side of All Saints Church. Silver Street was the main road from Pilgrim Street to Pandon. The street takes its name from the silver merchants who lived there in the late 17th century.

One of Newcastle's most famous historians, Henry Bourne, who was born in Newcastle in 1694, died of consumption in Silver Street on 16th February 1733. Bourne was for ten years the curate of All Hallows church. He was also the author of *History of Newcastle*, published after his death.

In 1821 eight yards of parapet wall surrounding the roof of All Saints Church was blown into Silver Street and a large urn was toppled from the steeple of the church into Butcher Bank causing much consternation to the residents.

An infamous character known as 'Jack the Beadle' lived in Silver Street in 1858. He would go into the churchyard at night and steal the lead lining from the coffins. His flickering lantern was spotted by the residents of Silver Street and he was caught red handed. He was sentenced to 18 months' hard labour.

In the late 19th century Silver Street was Newcastle's Italian Quarter.

6. Pilgrim Street and All Saints Church in 1964 before the building of the central motorway and Swan House completely changed the character of the area.

Silver Street lies behind All Saints. Dog Bank is in the foreground to the right. The large building at the top of Dog Bank is the Salvation Army Hostel. The railway viaduct was constructed in 1849 and widened in 1894.

Pilgrim Street was once described as 'the longest and fairest street in the town'. It was once a grand and fashionable street, and the main route from the old Tyne Bridge to the town.

The street is named for the pilgrims who walked along that road on their way to worship at St Mary's Chapel in Jesmond.

7. Dog Bank is a narrow lane leading from Pilgrim Street (where it joined Akenside Hill) to Broad Chare. Before the 19th century, the street was home to some of Newcastle's wealthy burgesses. The large photograph shows Dog Bank in around 1890, after the town's well-off folk had moved on. Around this time the street boasted five licensed lodging houses, two clothes dealers, one innkeeper, one beer retailer, a grocer, a glazier and a tinsmith. A labourer, Mr T. Ambrose, lived at No. 1 Dog Bank.

Above: the top of Dog Bank c.1950. On the left is the Salvation Army Hostel. The sign reads 'Good beds'.

8. Pandon was once the ancient town of Pampeden. In 1299, during the reign of Edward I, a grant was obtained to unite Pandon with Newcastle. The town wall was re-routed eastwards at Corner Tower through Pandon to Sallyport Tower (at Wall Knoll) and then down to the river at Sandgate. Pandon Dene, which remained outside the wall, was, according to Bourne a romantic area, frequented by strolling lovers. By the late 19th century, however, Pandon Dene was a tipping ground and described as 'full of rubbish'. During the 19th century Pandon developed into an area of warehouses serving the river trade. The 'Home for Destitute Boys' in Pandon House was a refuge for working boys. It was home to around 50 boys aged between 14 and 17 years until 1925.

9. Stockbridge looking south around 1880. Stockbridge was situated to the north of Broad Chare where Cowgate met Silver Street and Pandon (see illustration 1). It is thought to take its name from an ancient bridge that crossed a burn in Pandon Dene. The bridge was used to take livestock to slaughter. Stockbridge was the site of a fish market in the days when some fishing boats could sail up Pandon Burn far enough to unload.

The photograph shows Stockbridge in poor condition. The woman is standing at the bottom of Coburg Stairs and in the distance to the right is Blyth Nook. The road north from Stockbridge ran through Pandon Gate to Pandon Bank.

10. Keelmen's Hospital, City Road, in 1970. The hospital was built in 1701 at a cost of £2,000, using money from a fund which the keelmen had set up for old or infirm keelmen and their widows. At the beginning of the 20th century the Keelmen's Hospital contained 171 residents. It was the scene of a violent murder on New Year's Day, 1829, when Jane Jameson, a fishwife, murdered her mother in a drunken rage. Jameson's trial and execution drew huge crowds, partly because she was the first woman to be publicly hanged in Newcastle for 71 years. The brick quadrangle with its square clock tower (there was once a back clock tower too) has Dutch gables and a pantile roof. It is much restored.

11. This photograph shows Sandgate on 5 March 1897. The crowd has gathered beside a collapsed building at Wrangham's Entry. The original Sand Gate in the town wall was demolished in 1798 to widen the street. Sandgate ran parallel to the river and was the site of Paddy's Market where old clothes were sold. At the west end of the street near the Milk Market was the Sandgate Pant, or water fountain. It was built in 1891 to mark the centenary of the death of John Wesley who preached in the Sandgate area in 1742. At around this time the street contained numerous innkeepers, beer retailers, hairdressers, clothiers, and grocers, plus a butcher, a greengrocer, and a shipsmith. Miss M. McKenzie ran an 'eating-house' from 9 Sandgate. In the distance can be see a soap factory, and a large warehouse.

12. Milk Market, 1879, at the east end of Sandgate. This was the area where the townsfolk bought their milk and meat at a daily market. The Pant (water fountain) is in the foreground. Businesses operating from the Milk Market in this year included granaries run by Mr J. Pollard, four innkeepers, a grocer, a clothier, an eating-house, a tripe preparer, and an oil warehouse. At the end of the Milk Market was the Sandgate Midden where the town scavenger emptied his cart. The Midden was a festering heap of street sweepings and the waste from slaughter houses and other establishments, the contents of which was sold for manure and taken away by keel or farmer's cart.

13a, 13b. Cox Chare (Coxon's Chare), left, 1935, and Fenwick's Entry, right, 1967, are old names which survive on modern maps. The chares are said to have followed the lines of ancient strips of land. Fenwick's Entry had seven businesses operating from it in 1851. Many famous Tyneside personalities lived in and around the Quayside. In Love Lane, the last chare in this section of the Quayside, lived William Scott, father of both John, later Lord Eldon (born 4 June 1751, and later to elope with Bessie Surtees) and William, later Lord Stowell. William Scott was a coal fitter, effectively a middleman between the coal owners and the coal shippers. A large number of coal fitters in the 18th century operated from offices within the chares. There were four in Love Lane alone.

14. Broad Chare, 1967. Broad Chare, as its name suggests, was wider than most – wide enough for a cart to pass through (Broad Chare and Spicer Lane were amalgamated further widening the street). Mackenzie comments in his *History* 'Most of the old houses have been pulled down and lofty commodious warehouses erected in their place. A narrow flagged footpath runs up the west side, but it is neither a safe nor a pleasant passage.' Newcastle's Law Courts now occupy the site of the buildings on the right of the photograph.

15. Trinity House off Broad Chare, 1965. Trinity House is the home of the Guild of Masters and Mariners, one of the 15 'Bye Trades' of the Free Incorporated Companies of Newcastle. The site was purchased for the Guild in 1492. Trinity House is laid out around a secluded courtyard. Some of the buildings on this site date from the early 16th century. Other buildings, including a banqueting hall and entrance hall, were added in the late 18th century. Ship brokers and coal merchants traded from here for many years.

Today, Trinity House is the headquarters of Trinity House of Newcastle upon Tyne, a private corporation which has been dedicated to the welfare of seafarers since 1536.

16. Quayside c.1895. The floating wharf was moored opposite Broad Chare and Spicer Lane. The Plough Inn in Spicer Lane was reputedly the headquarters of the press gang in Newcastle in Napoleonic times. One tragic story tells of a young seaman called Stoddart, who was chased down Broad Chare by the press gang and tried to escape by swimming across to Gateshead. He was drowned in the Tyne. According to another story, a young man named Bell was being held by the press gang, but managed to swap clothes with his sister and make his escape.

17. Quayside, 1920. The Sunday market, a well-loved Newcastle tradition, is in full swing.

At this date the river played a vital part in Newcastle's trade with other parts of the country and the continent. A paddle steamer can be seen in the distance.

A section of the town wall, with many gates and a walkway at the top, once ran along the Quayside. During the reign of James I, the gates were ordered to be locked every night. Only one or two remained open to allow the Masters and seamen access to their ships. The gates were guarded all night long to prevent servants throwing ashes and other rubbish into the river.

By 1762 this section of the wall had outgrown its usefulness as a defensive structure. It was causing obstruction and was a hindrance to business on the Quay. George III granted authority for its demolition. Work began in January 1763 and the stones were used in building St Ann's Chapel.

18. The aftermath of the Quayside fire of 6 October 1854. Shortly before one o'clock in the morning, a fire was discovered in the factory of J. Wilson and Sons in Gateshead. A bonded warehouse adjacent to J. Wilson's premises containing many tons of materials including manganese, nitrate of soda, brimstone, guano, alum, arsenic and salt also ignited.

Despite the efforts of firemen and soldiers there was a terrible explosion, which threw burning material high into the air and blew out windows in shops on the Quayside. The missiles flew across the river and into houses on the Newcastle Quayside opposite. The result was a devastating fire. Because of the densely packed old buildings, the fire raged out of control. Fifteen people lost their lives and over 100 were injured.

Alexander Dobson, the talented son of Newcastle's celebrated architect, John Dobson, rushed to the scene of the fire to try to help the police and fire brigade. The confined area was crowded with people and Alexander was working within a few yards of the heart of the inferno. When tons of burning debris fell into the street Alexander and other brave volunteers were buried. He was just 26 years old.

Ironically, much of the redevelopment of the Quayside after the fire was designed by John Dobson. Elegant streets such as Queen Street, King Street and Lombard Street replaced the medieval chares of which only seven remain.

19. The Victorian buildings of the Quayside, 1971. The Customs House (just left of centre) is a fine example of Georgian architecture. It was completed in 1766 and built on the site of the former Peacock Inn. It was refronted in 1830. It replaced an older Customs House located at the western end of the Quayside, near Sandhill. The Customs House, next to the now demolished indoor market, is a listed building.

20. Queen Street, King Street and Lombard Street. The area between Dark Chare and Plummer Chare was badly damaged in the fire of 1854. It was redeveloped under the Newcastle upon Tyne Improvement Act of 1855. The remains of Grindon Chare, Blue Anchor Chare, Peppercorn Chare, Pallister Chare, Colvin's Chare and Hornsby Chare were torn down. Three elegant new streets, Queen Street, King Street and Lombard Street, designed by John Dobson, arose in their place. In 1863 the corporation built stone steps from Queen Street to the head of Akenside Hill to make it easier to move between the foot of Pilgrim Street and the Quayside. The photograph on the left dates from 1970 and looks along King Street, over Queen Street and up the steps to All Saints church at the foot of Pilgrim Street. On the right is the view down Lombard Street towards the Tyne in 1967. St Mary's Church in Gateshead can be seen across the river.

21. The official opening of the Tyne Bridge, 10 October 1928. In the late 18th and early 19th centuries, the centre of Newcastle had begun a gradual move away from the cramped waterside area towards higher ground. The opening of the road deck of the High Level Bridge in 1850 increased the process as incoming traffic could now avoid the Quayside. The new Tyne Bridge was another blow to the prominence of the Quayside as a commercial centre. Several buildings on the Quayside, including Cosyn's House, a grand Elizabethan residence named after 17th century Alderman John Cosyn, were demolished to make way for the bridge's giant supports.